Adult
MAD LIBS ▼

The world's greatest _pri___ game

We're Here, We're Queer,
We're Mad Libs

by Karl Marks

Mad Libs
An Imprint of Penguin Random House

MAD LIBS
An Imprint of Penguin Random House LLC

Concept created by Roger Price & Leonard Stern

Published by Mad Libs,
an imprint of Penguin Random House LLC,
345 Hudson Street, New York, New York 10014.
Printed in the USA.

ISBN 9780843172966

5 7 9 10 8 6 4

Adult MAD LIBS®

INSTRUCTIONS

The world's greatest _pride_ game

MAD LIBS® is a game for people who don't like games!
It can be played by one, two, three, four, or forty.

• RIDICULOUSLY SIMPLE DIRECTIONS

In this book, you'll find stories containing blank spaces where words are left out. One player, the READER, selects one of the stories. The READER shouldn't tell anyone what the story is about. Instead, the READER should ask the other players, the WRITERS, to give words to fill in the blank spaces in the story.

• TO PLAY

The READER asks each WRITER in turn to call out words—adjectives or nouns or whatever the spaces call for—and uses them to fill in the blank spaces in the story. The result is your very own MAD LIBS! Then, when the READER reads the completed MAD LIBS to the other players, they will discover they have written a story that is fantastic, screamingly funny, shocking, silly, crazy, or just plain dumb—depending on the words each WRITER called out.

• EXAMPLE (*Before* and *After*)

" _____ !" he said _____
    EXCLAMATION   ADVERB

as he jumped into his convertible _____ and
                                                    NOUN

drove off with his _____ wife.
                              ADJECTIVE

" _____*Ouch*_____ !" he said _____*stupidly*_____
    EXCLAMATION   ADVERB

as he jumped into his convertible _____*cat*_____ and
                                                    NOUN

drove off with his _____*brave*_____ wife.
                              ADJECTIVE

In case you have forgotten what adjectives, adverbs, nouns, and verbs are, here is a quick review:

An **ADJECTIVE** describes something or somebody. *Lumpy, soft, ugly, messy,* and *short* are adjectives.

An **ADVERB** tells how something is done. It modifies a verb and usually ends in "ly." *Modestly, stupidly, greedily,* and *carefully* are adverbs.

A **NOUN** is the name of a person, place, or thing. *Sidewalk, umbrella, bridle, bathtub,* and *nose* are nouns.

A **VERB** is an action word. *Run, pitch, jump,* and *swim* are verbs. Put the verbs in past tense if the directions say **PAST TENSE**. *Ran, pitched, jumped,* and *swam* are verbs in the past tense.

When we ask for **A PLACE**, we mean any sort of place: a country or city (*Spain, Cleveland*) or a room (*bathroom, kitchen*).

An **EXCLAMATION** or **SILLY WORD** is any sort of funny sound, gasp, grunt, or outcry, like *Wow!, Ouch!, Whomp!, Ick!,* and *Gadzooks!*

When we ask for specific words, like a **NUMBER**, a **COLOR**, an **ANIMAL**, or a **PART OF THE BODY**, we mean a word that is one of those things, like *seven, blue, horse,* or *head.*

When we ask for a **PLURAL**, it means more than one. For example, *cat* pluralized is *cats.*

Adult MAD LIBS ▼

The world's greatest _pride_ game

COMING OUT LETTER

MAD LIBS® is fun to play with friends, but you can also play it by yourself! To begin with, DO NOT look at the story on the page below. Fill in the blanks on this page with the words called for. Then, using the words you have selected, fill in the blank spaces in the story. Now you've created your own hilarious MAD LIBS® game!

NOUN _____

NOUN _____

PERSON IN ROOM (MALE) _____

PART OF THE BODY _____

ADJECTIVE _____

PLURAL NOUN _____

PLURAL NOUN _____

ADJECTIVE _____

ADJECTIVE _____

ADJECTIVE _____

PLURAL NOUN _____

PLURAL NOUN _____

NOUN _____

ADJECTIVE _____

PERSON IN ROOM (FEMALE) _____

NOUN _____

ADJECTIVE _____

COMING OUT LETTER

Dear Mom and _____,
    <u>NOUN</u>

Hi, it's me—your loving _____, _____.
    <u>NOUN</u>   <u>PERSON IN ROOM (MALE)</u>

My _____ is aching! I've wanted to talk to you about this
    <u>PART OF THE BODY</u>

for some time, but I get so _____ when I think about your
    <u>ADJECTIVE</u>

reaction that I haven't had the _____ to do it. Mom . . .
    <u>PLURAL NOUN</u>

Dad . . . I love _____! And as you may already know, I'm
    <u>PLURAL NOUN</u>

_____. I've known the _____ truth for some time
<u>ADJECTIVE</u>   <u>ADJECTIVE</u>

now. I know you might be _____ with _____ right
    <u>ADJECTIVE</u>   <u>PLURAL NOUN</u>

now, but hopefully in time you'll understand. Though you're not the

first _____ I've told, I wanted to be the _____ to
    <u>PLURAL NOUN</u>   <u>NOUN</u>

tell you before _____ Aunt _____ called to say, "I
    <u>ADJECTIVE</u>   <u>PERSON IN ROOM (FEMALE)</u>

told you your son was a big _____!"
    <u>NOUN</u>

Love,

Your _____ son
    <u>ADJECTIVE</u>

MAD LIBS® is fun to play with friends, but you can also play it by yourself! To begin with, DO NOT look at the story on the page below. Fill in the blanks on this page with the words called for. Then, using the words you have selected, fill in the blank spaces in the story. Now you've created your own hilarious MAD LIBS® game!

NOUN _____

ADJECTIVE _____

NOUN _____

NOUN _____

PART OF THE BODY_____

LETTER OF THE ALPHABET_____

ADJECTIVE _____

NOUN _____

PLURAL NOUN_____

ADJECTIVE _____

PLURAL NOUN_____

TYPE OF LIQUID _____

VERB ENDING IN "ING" _____

NOUN _____

PART OF THE BODY _____

PLURAL NOUN_____

ADJECTIVE _____

SILLY WORD _____

Adult MAD LIBS

The world's greatest _pride_ game

SAFE SEX 101: A LESSON IN PLAYING IT SAFE

You've finally started dating a hot _____. Now it's time to get
NOUN

_____ and take things to the next _____! But do
ADJECTIVE NOUN

you even know how to put a/an _____ on your _____?
NOUN PART OF THE BODY

No? Hold up—we've got to talk about ST-_____s! It's
LETTER OF THE ALPHABET

important to practice _____ sex so you can protect yourself
ADJECTIVE

and your _____-friend. One thing a lot of _____
NOUN PLURAL NOUN

do wrong is buy condoms that are too _____. Don't just buy
ADJECTIVE

Magnum _____ because you want to impress your date!
PLURAL NOUN

Additionally, make sure to use plenty of _____ when you are
TYPE OF LIQUID

_____, or it's possible that the _____ could break.
VERB ENDING IN "ING" NOUN

Another good rule of _____ is to get tested for _____
PART OF THE BODY PLURAL NOUN

before you get down and _____ with another person. You
ADJECTIVE

don't want to have to call your new sweetie to let him know he's got

_____!
SILLY WORD

Adult MAD LIBS

GAY ACTIVIST ACRONYMS: A GUIDE

The world's greatest _pride_ game

MAD LIBS® is fun to play with friends, but you can also play it by yourself! To begin with, DO NOT look at the story on the page below. Fill in the blanks on this page with the words called for. Then, using the words you have selected, fill in the blank spaces in the story. Now you've created your own hilarious MAD LIBS® game!

ADJECTIVE _____

PLURAL NOUN _____

NOUN _____

ADJECTIVE _____

ADJECTIVE _____

A PLACE _____

NOUN _____

NOUN _____

PLURAL NOUN _____

ADJECTIVE _____

ADJECTIVE _____

PLURAL NOUN _____

PLURAL NOUN _____

ADJECTIVE _____

PLURAL NOUN _____

ADJECTIVE _____

VERB ENDING IN "ING" _____

A PLACE _____

Adult
MAD LIBS
The world's greatest _pride_ game

GAY ACTIVIST ACRONYMS: A GUIDE

It can be _____ to keep track of all the nonprofit

ADJECTIVE

_____ marching in the Pride _____. Use this

PLURAL NOUN   NOUN

guide to who's who in the _____ activist community to mind

ADJECTIVE

your p's and q's . . . and your l's and g's and b's and t's . . .

- **HRC**—The Human Rights Campaign does advocacy on a/an

  _____ level. They are based in (the) _____.

ADJECTIVE   A PLACE

- **GLAAD**—The Gay & Lesbian _____ Against Defamation is

NOUN

  a media watch-_____ based in Los Angeles.

NOUN

- **PFLAG**—Parents, Families, and _____ of Lesbians and

PLURAL NOUN

  Gays is a/an _____ organization focused on _____

ADJECTIVE   ADJECTIVE

  family members of LGBT _____.

PLURAL NOUN

- **GLSEN**—The Gay, Lesbian & Straight Education Network works

  with educators and _____ to make schools

PLURAL NOUN

  _____ for young LGBT _____.

ADJECTIVE   PLURAL NOUN

- **National Gay and Lesbian Task Force**—A/An _____

ADJECTIVE

  grassroots organization focused on _____ gay rights in

VERB ENDING IN "ING"

  (the) _____.

A PLACE

Adult
MAD LIBS®
▼

CUBS AND OTTERS AND BEARS, OH MY!

The world's greatest _pride_ game

MAD LIBS® is fun to play with friends, but you can also play it by yourself! To begin with, DO NOT look at the story on the page below. Fill in the blanks on this page with the words called for. Then, using the words you have selected, fill in the blank spaces in the story. Now you've created your own hilarious MAD LIBS® game!

ADJECTIVE _____

ADJECTIVE _____

NOUN _____

EXCLAMATION _____

VERB _____

PLURAL NOUN _____

CELEBRITY (MALE) _____

PLURAL NOUN _____

VERB ENDING IN "ING" _____

ADJECTIVE _____

VERB _____

PLURAL NOUN _____

PART OF THE BODY _____

VERB _____

NOUN _____

NOUN _____

PLURAL NOUN _____

ADJECTIVE _____

It's your first time at a/an _____ bar, and a/an _____

ADJECTIVE   ADJECTIVE

lesbian with her _____ off calls you an otter. What the

NOUN

_____ is an otter, anyway? This list will sort you out before

EXCLAMATION

you accidentally _____ the bears.

VERB

- **Babydykes**—These _____ are younger lesbians who tend to

PLURAL NOUN

  dress like _____.

CELEBRITY (MALE)

- **Bulldykes**—More mature _____ with a penchant for

PLURAL NOUN

  _____ fights with other bulldykes.

VERB ENDING IN "ING"

- **Bears**—Big _____ dudes who love to _____.

ADJECTIVE   VERB

- **Drag Queens**—Men who wear women's _____ and tons of

PLURAL NOUN

  _____ makeup, and love to _____ onstage!

PART OF THE BODY   VERB

- **Gym Queens**—Shaved, oiled, and tan, these muscle heads do

  nothing but lift weights and drink _____ shakes.

NOUN

- **Lipstick Lesbians**—These ladies get all their _____ advice

NOUN

  from *The L Word*. Watch out for these fatally femme _____.

PLURAL NOUN

- **Otters**—Skinny, hairy gay guys who don't seem to fit in at the local

  _____ bar.

ADJECTIVE

ONLINE DATING DOS AND DON'TS 4 GAYZ

MAD LIBS® is fun to play with friends, but you can also play it by yourself! To begin with, DO NOT look at the story on the page below. Fill in the blanks on this page with the words called for. Then, using the words you have selected, fill in the blank spaces in the story. Now you've created your own hilarious MAD LIBS® game!

ADJECTIVE _____

PART OF THE BODY _____

ADJECTIVE _____

NUMBER _____

ADJECTIVE _____

ADJECTIVE _____

PLURAL NOUN _____

NOUN _____

PLURAL NOUN _____

NUMBER _____

NOUN _____

NOUN _____

PLURAL NOUN _____

NOUN _____

ADJECTIVE _____

PLURAL NOUN _____

NUMBER _____

CELEBRITY _____

Your _____ new boyfriend just changed his status to "In
_{ADJECTIVE}

a Relationship" on _____-book, but your _____
_{PART OF THE BODY}   _{ADJECTIVE}

friend just showed you your boyfriend's Grindr profile, and he is

only _____ feet away and "Looking." Whether you're the
_{NUMBER}

_____ boyfriend or the _____ victim, use these dos
_{ADJECTIVE}   _{ADJECTIVE}

and don'ts to navigate the online dating scene.

- **Do** tell your closest _____ about your new _____
_{PLURAL NOUN}   _{NOUN}

  before you post it to Facebook, so no one's _____ get hurt.
  _{PLURAL NOUN}

- **Don't** make your "Single" status public only _____ hours
_{NUMBER}

  after breaking up with your ex-_____.
  _{NOUN}

- **Do** tell the truth in your online _____, but don't exaggerate.
_{NOUN}

- **Don't** log on to Grindr looking for _____ when you're in the
_{PLURAL NOUN}

  same neighborhood as your current _____'s best friend.
  _{NOUN}

- **Do** use lighting and angles to take _____ pics of yourself that
_{ADJECTIVE}

  show off your best _____.
  _{PLURAL NOUN}

- **Don't** use Photoshop to try to make yourself look _____
_{NUMBER}

  years younger and exactly like _____.
  _{CELEBRITY}

Adult
MAD LIBS ▼

The world's greatest _pride_ game

LESBIAN POTLUCK: A MENU

MAD LIBS® is fun to play with friends, but you can also play it by yourself! To begin with, DO NOT look at the story on the page below. Fill in the blanks on this page with the words called for. Then, using the words you have selected, fill in the blank spaces in the story. Now you've created your own hilarious MAD LIBS® game!

PERSON IN ROOM (FEMALE) _____

VERB ENDING IN "ING" _____

ADJECTIVE _____

ADJECTIVE _____

PLURAL NOUN _____

PERSON IN ROOM (FEMALE) _____

PERSON IN ROOM (FEMALE) _____

COLOR _____

NOUN _____

TYPE OF LIQUID _____

ADJECTIVE _____

PLURAL NOUN _____

PLURAL NOUN _____

NOUN _____

ADVERB _____

ADJECTIVE _____

NUMBER _____

Adult MAD LIBS

The world's greatest _pride_ game

LESBIAN POTLUCK: A MENU

You have invited _____ and all her lesbian friends over for
_{PERSON IN ROOM (FEMALE)}

a big old potluck after _____ *The Real L Word* together. But
_{VERB ENDING IN "ING"}

what to make? Here's a list of _____ dishes that are sure to
_{ADJECTIVE}

impress all your _____ friends.
_{ADJECTIVE}

You can't go wrong with serving _____ as an appetizer.
_{PLURAL NOUN}

Since Lucy, _____, and _____ don't eat
_{PERSON IN ROOM (FEMALE)}   _{PERSON IN ROOM (FEMALE)}

_____ meat, this healthy dish is sure to please everyone.
_{COLOR}

Everyone loves a salad, so pick up some greens from your local

_____ market. Use some _____ and vinegar to
_{NOUN}   _{TYPE OF LIQUID}

make your own _____ salad dressing to bring out the flavors
_{ADJECTIVE}

of the _____!
_{PLURAL NOUN}

For the main course, stick with the vegetarian theme and sauté

some tasty _____ and serve them over a/an _____
_{PLURAL NOUN}   _{NOUN}

of couscous. This dish serves a large group _____, and
_{ADVERB}

you'll have more than enough for your _____ guests to have
_{ADJECTIVE}

_____ or more helpings.
_{NUMBER}

MAD LIBS® is fun to play with friends, but you can also play it by yourself! To begin with, DO NOT look at the story on the page below. Fill in the blanks on this page with the words called for. Then, using the words you have selected, fill in the blank spaces in the story. Now you've created your own hilarious MAD LIBS® game!

PLURAL NOUN _____

NOUN_____

PLURAL NOUN _____

ADJECTIVE_____

ADJECTIVE _____

ADJECTIVE _____

ADJECTIVE _____

A PLACE (PLURAL)_____

ADJECTIVE_____

NOUN_____

PLURAL NOUN _____

NOUN_____

PLURAL NOUN _____

VERB ENDING IN "ING" _____

ADJECTIVE _____

Straight people love gay bars! There's no pressure to flirt with

_____, and you can dance the _____ away without
PLURAL NOUN   NOUN

being bothered. But gays love labels, so take this quiz to find out how

you fit in.

Are you a guy who hangs out with _____, has lots of
                                        PLURAL NOUN

_____ friends, and would rather wear a/an _____
ADJECTIVE   ADJECTIVE

flannel shirt to a fancy dinner than a/an _____ suit? You
                                            ADJECTIVE

might be a **stag hag**.

Are you a girl who loves _____ guys because they are so
                              ADJECTIVE

funny and fabulously _____? Do you like to hang out in gay
                        ADJECTIVE

_____ because you feel safe and love the _____ music
A PLACE (PLURAL)   ADJECTIVE

the DJs play there? If you don't have a best gay _____, but
                                                    NOUN

you totally support gay _____, then you might be a **fruit fly**.
                          PLURAL NOUN

Do you love every gay _____ that you meet? Are all
                            NOUN

your best _____ gay? Would you rather spend your time
            PLURAL NOUN

_____ with all the _____ men in your life than
VERB ENDING IN "ING"   ADJECTIVE

shopping with your girlfriends at the mall? You're probably a **fag hag**.

MAD LIBS® is fun to play with friends, but you can also play it by yourself! To begin with, DO NOT look at the story on the page below. Fill in the blanks on this page with the words called for. Then, using the words you have selected, fill in the blank spaces in the story. Now you've created your own hilarious MAD LIBS® game!

ADJECTIVE _____

TYPE OF LIQUID _____

ADJECTIVE _____

ADVERB _____

COLOR _____

ANIMAL (PLURAL) _____

NUMBER _____

ADJECTIVE _____

ADJECTIVE _____

PLURAL NOUN _____

TYPE OF LIQUID _____

NOUN _____

PERSON IN ROOM (MALE) _____

TYPE OF LIQUID _____

NUMBER _____

LETTER OF THE ALPHABET _____

GET YOUR GAY DRINK ON

Vodka before beer, never queer . . . wait, that's not right. It's important to serve the _____ amount of _____ at
ADJECTIVE   TYPE OF LIQUID

your party so your friends get _____ enough to have fun but
ADJECTIVE

still make it home _____.
ADVERB

- **Vodka**—Gays can drink _____ Goose like it's water and
COLOR

  they're thirsty _____ about to cross the desert. Don't
ANIMAL (PLURAL)

  run out!

- **Gin**—If you're inviting anyone over _____ to your party,
NUMBER

  they'll want to drink this _____ liquor and talk about the
ADJECTIVE

  _____ old days when gay people knew how to party!
ADJECTIVE

- **Whiskey**—You might have some hipster _____ show up,
PLURAL NOUN

  and everyone knows they only drink _____ that matches
TYPE OF LIQUID

  their ironic facial _____.
NOUN

- **Beer**—You'll need this for your friend _____, who only
PERSON IN ROOM (MALE)

  drinks _____ to show everyone how "straight" he is. But
TYPE OF LIQUID

  it's good to have a case or _____ of PB-_____ in
NUMBER   LETTER OF THE ALPHABET

  case some lesbians show up, too.

Adult
▼
MAD LIBS®

GAY AND REPUBLICAN: A MANIFESTO

The world's greatest _pride_ game

MAD LIBS® is fun to play with friends, but you can also play it by yourself! To begin with, DO NOT look at the story on the page below. Fill in the blanks on this page with the words called for. Then, using the words you have selected, fill in the blank spaces in the story.

Now you've created your own hilarious MAD LIBS® game!

PERSON IN ROOM _____

PLURAL NOUN _____

ADJECTIVE _____

ADJECTIVE _____

CELEBRITY (MALE) _____

ADJECTIVE _____

PLURAL NOUN _____

ADJECTIVE _____

PLURAL NOUN _____

ADJECTIVE _____

ADVERB _____

PLURAL NOUN _____

ADJECTIVE _____

PLURAL NOUN _____

NOUN _____

ADVERB _____

PLURAL NOUN _____

Adult MAD LIBS

The world's greatest _pride_ game

GAY AND REPUBLICAN: A MANIFESTO

"I, _____, swear to uphold the _____ of the
     PERSON IN ROOM   PLURAL NOUN

_____ Old Party."
   ADJECTIVE

Just because I'm gay doesn't mean I can't attend _____ parties
                                                        ADJECTIVE

in the Hamptons and vote for _____ for president. And
                                  CELEBRITY (MALE)

just because I like _____ government doesn't mean I don't like
                          ADJECTIVE

large _____, too. Being an openly _____ Republican
          PLURAL NOUN   ADJECTIVE

doesn't mean I can't advocate equal rights for all _____
                                                         PLURAL NOUN

and lesbians. I'm fiscally _____ and _____ liberal,
                                 ADJECTIVE   ADVERB

and there's room for all _____ in the GOP. I vote for
                               PLURAL NOUN

_____ candidates based on their adherence to conservative
   ADJECTIVE

_____, and I think for myself. And just because I'm
   PLURAL NOUN

conservative with _____-sheets doesn't mean I don't know
                         NOUN

how to _____ rock it under the bed-_____!
            ADVERB   PLURAL NOUN

Adult
MAD LIBS
The world's greatest _pride_ game
DON'T BRING YOUR U-HAUL

MAD LIBS® is fun to play with friends, but you can also play it by yourself! To begin with, DO NOT look at the story on the page below. Fill in the blanks on this page with the words called for. Then, using the words you have selected, fill in the blank spaces in the story. Now you've created your own hilarious MAD LIBS® game!

ADJECTIVE _____

ADJECTIVE _____

VERB _____

A PLACE _____

PLURAL NOUN _____

PLURAL NOUN _____

NUMBER _____

ANIMAL _____

NUMBER _____

PLURAL NOUN _____

ADVERB _____

PART OF THE BODY _____

ARTICLE OF CLOTHING _____

OCCUPATION _____

PERSON IN ROOM (MALE) _____

PERSON IN ROOM (FEMALE) _____

Adult
MAD LIBS ▼

The world's greatest _pride_ game

DON'T BRING YOUR U-HAUL

Here's a/an _____ guide to the lesbian first date:

ADJECTIVE

• **Do** go somewhere with a/an _____ atmosphere where you

ADJECTIVE

can _____ and get to know each other.

VERB

• **Don't** go to a lesbian _____ where you're sure to run into

A PLACE

lots of ex-_____. Can you say awkward?

PLURAL NOUN

• **Do** talk about music, film, and _____.

PLURAL NOUN

• **Don't** talk about the _____ other girls you've dated over the

NUMBER

past year.

• **Do** talk about your favorite _____.

ANIMAL

• **Don't** bring photos of your _____ cats and talk about the

NUMBER

_____ they eat.

PLURAL NOUN

• **Do** laugh at her jokes _____, and gently touch her

ADVERB

_____ to show interest.

PART OF THE BODY

• **Don't** try to stick your hand under her _____.

ARTICLE OF CLOTHING

• **Do** mention your job as a/an _____.

OCCUPATION

• **Don't** tell her about your crushes on your coworkers,

_____ and _____.

PERSON IN ROOM (MALE)　　　PERSON IN ROOM (FEMALE)

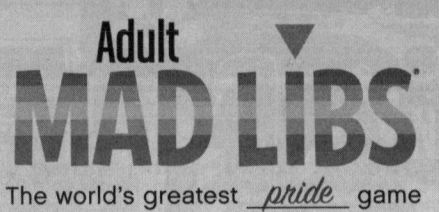

Adult MAD LIBS®

WHAT'S THE TEA?: A GOSSIP COLUMN

The world's greatest _pride_ game

MAD LIBS® is fun to play with friends, but you can also play it by yourself! To begin with, DO NOT look at the story on the page below. Fill in the blanks on this page with the words called for. Then, using the words you have selected, fill in the blank spaces in the story. Now you've created your own hilarious MAD LIBS® game!

EXCLAMATION _____

CELEBRITY (FEMALE) _____

FIRST NAME _____

NOUN _____

NOUN _____

COLOR _____

CELEBRITY (MALE) _____

PERSON IN ROOM (FEMALE) _____

PLURAL NOUN _____

SILLY WORD _____

ADVERB _____

VERB ENDING IN "ING" _____

ADJECTIVE _____

NOUN _____

NUMBER _____

VERB ENDING IN "ING" _____

Adult MAD LIBS

The world's greatest _pride_ game

WHAT'S THE TEA?: A GOSSIP COLUMN

_____, gurrrlll! Did you see what _____ wore to the
EXCLAMATION · CELEBRITY (FEMALE)

_____ Awards this year? What a tragic _____ she is.
FIRST NAME · NOUN

That faux-_____ coat! And those mismatched _____
NOUN · COLOR

heels! She's a mess! And can you believe Miss Thing arrived with

_____ and _____, when everyone knows they
CELEBRITY (MALE) · PERSON IN ROOM (FEMALE)

are total _____! Gurrrlll, please! I mean, we all loved her
PLURAL NOUN

album _____, but she _____ sold out when she
SILLY WORD · ADVERB

started _____ with DJ _____. I just hope tickets
VERB ENDING IN "ING" · ADJECTIVE

for her next _____ aren't, like, _____ dollars again.
NOUN · NUMBER

She is not fierce enough to be _____ her fans like that!
VERB ENDING IN "ING"

Adult

MAD LIBS ▼

A SECRET LOVE LETTER FROM HONEST ABE

The world's greatest _pride_ game

MAD LIBS® is fun to play with friends, but you can also play it by yourself! To begin with, DO NOT look at the story on the page below. Fill in the blanks on this page with the words called for. Then, using the words you have selected, fill in the blank spaces in the story. Now you've created your own hilarious MAD LIBS® game!

ADJECTIVE _____

NOUN _____

PERSON IN ROOM (MALE) _____

ADJECTIVE _____

PLURAL NOUN _____

NOUN _____

NOUN _____

ADJECTIVE _____

ADJECTIVE _____

NOUN _____

ADJECTIVE _____

NOUN _____

PERSON IN ROOM (MALE) _____

NOUN _____

VERB _____

PART OF THE BODY _____

ADVERB _____

NOUN _____

Adult MAD LIBS

A SECRET LOVE LETTER FROM HONEST ABE

The world's greatest _pride_ game

Everyone knows Abe Lincoln was totally _____! Here's the
ADJECTIVE

proof: a letter professing his _____ for his "personal friend,"
NOUN

_____.
PERSON IN ROOM (MALE)

Do not be _____ in regard to what my real _____ toward
ADJECTIVE   PLURAL NOUN

you are. Perhaps any other _____ would know enough without
NOUN

further _____, but I consider it my _____ right to
NOUN   ADJECTIVE

plead ignorance, and your _____ duty to allow the plea.
ADJECTIVE

Do not understand by this _____ that I wish to cut your
NOUN

_____ acquaintance. What I do wish is that our
ADJECTIVE

further _____ should depend upon _____.
NOUN   PERSON IN ROOM (MALE)

If you feel yourself in any _____ bound to me, I am now
NOUN

willing to _____ you, provided you wish it; while, on the
VERB

other _____, I am willing and even anxious to bind you
PART OF THE BODY

_____, if I can be convinced that it will in any degree add to
ADVERB

your _____.
NOUN

Your friend,

A. Lincoln

Adult
▼
MAD LIBS®

CELEBRITY GOSSIP FROM THE *GARLIC*

The world's greatest _pride_ game

MAD LIBS® is fun to play with friends, but you can also play it by yourself! To begin with, DO NOT look at the story on the page below. Fill in the blanks on this page with the words called for. Then, using the words you have selected, fill in the blank spaces in the story.

Now you've created your own hilarious MAD LIBS® game!

ADJECTIVE _____

ADJECTIVE _____

NOUN _____

CELEBRITY (MALE) _____

A PLACE _____

PERSON IN ROOM (MALE) _____

PLURAL NOUN _____

TYPE OF FOOD _____

PLURAL NOUN _____

PART OF THE BODY (PLURAL) _____

NOUN _____

NOUN _____

VERB ENDING IN "ING" _____

NOUN _____

ADVERB _____

Adult
MAD LIBS®
The world's greatest _pride_ game

CELEBRITY GOSSIP
FROM THE *GARLIC*

A special post from the *Garlic*, a magazine for _____ readers
ADJECTIVE

who are too _____ for other vegetable satire magazines.
ADJECTIVE

Rumors continue to fly about the sexual _____ *of*
NOUN

_____ *. He was recently seen at (the)* _____
CELEBRITY (MALE) A PLACE

with _____ *. No photographs have surfaced, but several*
PERSON IN ROOM (MALE)

_____ *have confirmed the couple dined on* _____
PLURAL NOUN TYPE OF FOOD

and _____ *at the restaurant. Upon leaving, they were seen*
PLURAL NOUN

holding each other's _____ *, and they shared an intense*
PART OF THE BODY (PLURAL)

_____ *before getting into a limo. Sources connected with the*
NOUN

_____ *tell the* Garlic *the two are "very close" to* _____
NOUN VERB ENDING IN "ING"

out publicly as a/an _____ *. We're told the celebrity is planning*
NOUN

to announce the relationship _____ *this week.*
ADVERB

From ADULT MAD LIBS®: We're Here, We're Queer, We're Mad Libs • Copyright © 2013 by Penguin Random House LLC.

Adult
MAD LIBS
The world's greatest _pride_ game

TIPS FOR YOUR
FIRST TIME IN DRAG

MAD LIBS® is fun to play with friends, but you can also play it by yourself! To begin with, DO NOT look at the story on the page below. Fill in the blanks on this page with the words called for. Then, using the words you have selected, fill in the blank spaces in the story. Now you've created your own hilarious MAD LIBS® game!

NOUN _____

ADJECTIVE _____

VERB _____

NOUN _____

PART OF THE BODY (PLURAL) _____

ADVERB _____

VERB _____

ARTICLE OF CLOTHING _____

VERB _____

PLURAL NOUN _____

ADJECTIVE _____

NOUN _____

ADJECTIVE _____

PART OF THE BODY (PLURAL) _____

ADJECTIVE _____

NOUN _____

COLOR _____

Adult
▼
MAD LIBS®

The world's greatest _pride_ game

TIPS FOR YOUR
FIRST TIME IN DRAG

Pull the shades, lock the front _____, and turn your inner diva
                                    NOUN

out! Here are some _____ hints for your first time in drag.
                     ADJECTIVE

Makeup: First, you'll want to _____ your face with
                                    VERB

foundation. Go for a theatrical look! Make sure you use

_____-liner and mascara for your _____. Apply
   NOUN   PART OF THE BODY (PLURAL)

lipstick _____ to your lips. And don't forget to _____
          ADVERB   VERB

those cheeks with blush!

Outfit: Three words: over-the-top. Find a/an _____ that
                                                  ARTICLE OF CLOTHING

sparkles! Be sure there is plenty of room to _____ your bra
                                               VERB

with _____.
      PLURAL NOUN

Wigs: No self-R-E-S-P-E-C-T-ing drag queen can lip-synch to Aretha

without a fabulously _____ wig. Go to the _____
                      ADJECTIVE   NOUN

store and find something _____ that ignites your look!
                          ADJECTIVE

Shoes: Heels, not flats. Guys have big _____, so finding
                                            PART OF THE BODY (PLURAL)

fabulous heels can be _____. The best option: Buy shoes
                       ADJECTIVE

from your local discount _____ warehouse and spray-paint
                          NOUN

them bright _____.
             COLOR

MAD LIBS® is fun to play with friends, but you can also play it by yourself! To begin with, DO NOT look at the story on the page below. Fill in the blanks on this page with the words called for. Then, using the words you have selected, fill in the blank spaces in the story. Now you've created your own hilarious MAD LIBS® game!

ADJECTIVE _____

ADJECTIVE _____

NOUN _____

PERSON IN ROOM (FEMALE) _____

PERSON IN ROOM (FEMALE) _____

ADVERB _____

NOUN _____

PLURAL NOUN _____

NOUN _____

ADJECTIVE _____

ADVERB _____

PLURAL NOUN _____

PLURAL NOUN _____

PART OF THE BODY (PLURAL) _____

VERB _____

NOUN _____

NOUN _____

VERB _____

Adult MAD LIBS

HERS AND HERS: LESBIAN WEDDING VOWS

The world's greatest _pride_ game

Saying "I do" is a/an _____ commitment. Here are some

ADJECTIVE

totally _____ wedding vows to help you commemorate your

ADJECTIVE

special _____ .

NOUN

_____ and _____ , we are gathered here

PERSON IN ROOM (FEMALE)   PERSON IN ROOM (FEMALE)

_____ to witness the love and respect that you have for

ADVERB

each other.

Are you entering into this _____ freely, voluntarily, and

NOUN

without any _____ ?

PLURAL NOUN

Happiness in _____ is not something that just happens.

NOUN

A/An _____ marriage must be worked on _____ .

ADJECTIVE   ADVERB

The little _____ are the big _____ .

PLURAL NOUN   PLURAL NOUN

It is never being too old to hold _____ .

PART OF THE BODY (PLURAL)

It is remembering to say "I _____ you" at least once a day.

VERB

It is not only marrying the right _____ ,

NOUN

it is being the right _____ .

NOUN

If you agree, say "I _____ !"

VERB

From ADULT MAD LIBS®: We're Here, We're Queer, We're Mad Libs • Copyright © 2013 by Penguin Random House LLC.

MAD LIBS® is fun to play with friends, but you can also play it by yourself! To begin with, DO NOT look at the story on the page below. Fill in the blanks on this page with the words called for. Then, using the words you have selected, fill in the blank spaces in the story. Now you've created your own hilarious MAD LIBS® game!

PART OF THE BODY (PLURAL) _____

VERB (PAST TENSE)_____

PLURAL NOUN _____

TYPE OF LIQUID_____

NOUN _____

NOUN _____

ADJECTIVE _____

PART OF THE BODY_____

EXCLAMATION _____

NOUN _____

PART OF THE BODY_____

TYPE OF LIQUID _____

NUMBER _____

ADJECTIVE_____

Adult
MAD LIBS®
The world's greatest _pride_ game

GAY BEACH BODY GUIDE

You've blasted your _____, you've _____ your

                PART OF THE BODY (PLURAL)   VERB (PAST TENSE)

abs, and you've been eating nothing but _____ and drinking

                                                PLURAL NOUN

gallons of _____ to stay hydrated. What else can you do to

                TYPE OF LIQUID

get your _____ beach-ready? Some people like to accentuate

                NOUN

their _____ by removing _____ body hair. You can

             NOUN   ADJECTIVE

always try shaving, but be sure not to get the razor too close to your

_____! Waxing is also an option, but—_____! It

PART OF THE BODY   EXCLAMATION

hurts. Tanning also adds a healthy _____ to your appearance,

                                     NOUN

but don't overexpose your _____. Sunburns aren't sexy!

                              PART OF THE BODY

You might want to try a tanning _____ that lasts for

                                      TYPE OF LIQUID

_____ hours. It's a much better choice, especially if you want

      NUMBER

to keep your skin _____ for years of gay beach time to come!

                  ADJECTIVE

Adult
MAD LIBS ▼
GAYDAR

The world's greatest _pride_ game

MAD LIBS® is fun to play with friends, but you can also play it by yourself! To begin with, DO NOT look at the story on the page below. Fill in the blanks on this page with the words called for. Then, using the words you have selected, fill in the blank spaces in the story. Now you've created your own hilarious MAD LIBS® game!

FIRST NAME (FEMALE) _____

VERB (PAST TENSE) _____

ADJECTIVE _____

COLOR _____

CELEBRITY (FEMALE) _____

ADJECTIVE _____

ADJECTIVE _____

SILLY WORD _____

TYPE OF LIQUID _____

ARTICLE OF CLOTHING (PLURAL) _____

PLURAL NOUN _____

CELEBRITY (FEMALE) _____

CELEBRITY (MALE) _____

OCCUPATION _____

TYPE OF FOOD _____

NUMBER _____

ARTICLE OF CLOTHING (PLURAL) _____

Adult
MAD LIBS ▼
GAYDAR

The world's greatest _pride_ game

He reads _____ magazine, but he _____ football
           FIRST NAME (FEMALE)   VERB (PAST TENSE)

in college. He's got _____ style and wears _____
                     ADJECTIVE   COLOR

socks, but he talks about _____ like he's in love. Hone
                             CELEBRITY (FEMALE)

your gaydar with this guide to knowing who's _____ and
                                               ADJECTIVE

who's _____.
      ADJECTIVE

- He prefers a bottle of Veuve _____ to a keg of
                                       SILLY WORD

  _____. **Gay!**
    TYPE OF LIQUID

- He wears ill-fitting _____ and hates talking about his
                        ARTICLE OF CLOTHING (PLURAL)

  _____. **Straight!**
  PLURAL NOUN

- He loves _____ and thinks _____ is in the
           CELEBRITY (FEMALE)   CELEBRITY (MALE)

  closet. **Gay!**

- He's got a great job as a/an _____ at the factory and
                              OCCUPATION

  loves Mom's homemade _____. **Straight!**
                        TYPE OF FOOD

- He owns _____ pairs of shoes but doesn't always wear
          NUMBER

  _____. **Good luck!**
  ARTICLE OF CLOTHING (PLURAL)

Adult
MAD LIBS ▼

The world's greatest _pride_ game

WE'RE HERE, WE'RE QUEER

MAD LIBS® is fun to play with friends, but you can also play it by yourself! To begin with, DO NOT look at the story on the page below. Fill in the blanks on this page with the words called for. Then, using the words you have selected, fill in the blank spaces in the story. Now you've created your own hilarious MAD LIBS® game!

PLURAL NOUN _____

PLURAL NOUN _____

ADJECTIVE _____

NOUN _____

PLURAL NOUN _____

ADJECTIVE _____

ADJECTIVE _____

PLURAL NOUN _____

SAME PLURAL NOUN _____

NOUN _____

SAME NOUN _____

NOUN _____

SAME NOUN _____

ADJECTIVE _____

VERB _____

SAME ADJECTIVE _____

SAME VERB _____

MAD LIBS

Adult

The world's greatest _pride_ game

WE'RE HERE, WE'RE QUEER

When it comes to marching in _____ and organizing political
PLURAL NOUN

_____, the _____ community knows how to be seen.
PLURAL NOUN   ADJECTIVE

Before marching in your local Pride _____, be sure to brush
NOUN

up on these important march _____:
PLURAL NOUN

"We're _____! We're _____! Get used to it!"
ADJECTIVE   ADJECTIVE

"Out of the closet and into the _____! Out of the closet and
PLURAL NOUN

into the _____!"
SAME PLURAL NOUN

"What do we want? _____! When do we want it? NOW!
NOUN

What do we want? _____! When do we want it? NOW!"
SAME NOUN

"Hey, hey! Ho, ho! _____ has got to go! Hey, hey! Ho, ho!
NOUN

_____ has got to go!"
SAME NOUN

"We're here! We're queer! We're _____! Don't _____
ADJECTIVE   VERB

with us! We're here! We're queer! We're _____! Don't
SAME ADJECTIVE

_____ with us!"
SAME VERB

Adult ▼ MAD LIBS®

HANKIE CODE

The world's greatest _pride_ game

MAD LIBS® is fun to play with friends, but you can also play it by yourself! To begin with, DO NOT look at the story on the page below. Fill in the blanks on this page with the words called for. Then, using the words you have selected, fill in the blank spaces in the story. Now you've created your own hilarious MAD LIBS® game!

ADJECTIVE _____

ARTICLE OF CLOTHING _____

NOUN _____

NOUN _____

A PLACE _____

COLOR _____

PART OF THE BODY_____

PART OF THE BODY_____

COLOR _____

VERB ENDING IN "ING" _____

OCCUPATION _____

NUMBER _____

PLURAL NOUN _____

SAME PLURAL NOUN _____

SAME PLURAL NOUN _____

Do you know your hankie code? In the 1970s, gay men used a code of colored handkerchiefs to identify one another and their _____ proclivities. Use this guide so you don't get caught
ADJECTIVE

unawares.

- If he's got a black handkerchief hanging out of his _____, he might call you _____ while you handcuff
ARTICLE OF CLOTHING   NOUN

  him to your _____ in (the) _____.
NOUN   A PLACE

- A/An _____ hankie means he wants to put your
COLOR

  _____ in his _____ and probably admires Monica
PART OF THE BODY   PART OF THE BODY

  Lewinsky for her taste in _____ dresses.
COLOR

- If he's _____ a green hankie, you better have a great job
VERB ENDING IN "ING"

  as a/an _____, because it's going to take _____
OCCUPATION   NUMBER

  dollars to get anything started with this stud.

- Orange is bright for a reason. This guy is up for _____,
PLURAL NOUN

  _____, and more _____—anytime, anywhere!
SAME PLURAL NOUN   SAME PLURAL NOUN

Adult MAD LIBS®

The world's greatest _pride_ game

HISTORY OF PRIDE: THE STONEWALL RIOTS

MAD LIBS® is fun to play with friends, but you can also play it by yourself! To begin with, DO NOT look at the story on the page below. Fill in the blanks on this page with the words called for. Then, using the words you have selected, fill in the blank spaces in the story. Now you've created your own hilarious MAD LIBS® game!

ADJECTIVE _____

ADJECTIVE _____

ADJECTIVE _____

PLURAL NOUN _____

CELEBRITY (FEMALE) _____

PLURAL NOUN _____

ARTICLE OF CLOTHING (PLURAL) _____

PLURAL NOUN _____

VERB ENDING IN "ING" _____

NOUN _____

PLURAL NOUN _____

A PLACE _____

ADJECTIVE _____

ADJECTIVE _____

ADVERB _____

ADJECTIVE _____

ADJECTIVE _____

PLURAL NOUN _____

ADULT MAD LIBS

The world's greatest *pride* game

HISTORY OF PRIDE: THE STONEWALL RIOTS

After years of police raids on _____ bars, history was made at
ADJECTIVE

the Stonewall Inn, a gay bar in New York City. In the _____
ADJECTIVE

hours of June 28, 1969, during a/an _____ police bust, the
ADJECTIVE

gays, lesbians, and drag _____ fought back. Maybe it was
PLURAL NOUN

_____'s recent death, or maybe the _____ had
CELEBRITY (FEMALE)   PLURAL NOUN

just had enough. Maybe it was the _____ worn by the
ARTICLE OF CLOTHING (PLURAL)

plainclothes police _____. But this time, everyone said, "No!"
PLURAL NOUN

and started _____. No one knows who threw the first
VERB ENDING IN "ING"

_____, but soon hundreds of _____ gathered in front
NOUN   PLURAL NOUN

of (the) _____. The _____ political organizations got
A PLACE   ADJECTIVE

involved and organized marches and protests lasting for weeks. Many

of today's _____ pride events are held _____ in June to
ADJECTIVE   ADVERB

commemorate the Stonewall Riots. So, be proud, be _____,
ADJECTIVE

and remember what your _____ history teacher in high
ADJECTIVE

school always said: "_____ shape the course of history."
PLURAL NOUN

MAD LIBS® is fun to play with friends, but you can also play it by yourself! To begin with, DO NOT look at the story on the page below. Fill in the blanks on this page with the words called for. Then, using the words you have selected, fill in the blank spaces in the story. Now you've created your own hilarious MAD LIBS® game!

PLURAL NOUN _____

ADJECTIVE _____

ADJECTIVE _____

NOUN _____

TYPE OF LIQUID _____

PLURAL NOUN _____

PLURAL NOUN _____

LETTER OF THE ALPHABET _____

ARTICLE OF CLOTHING _____

CELEBRITY (FEMALE) _____

PLURAL NOUN _____

NOUN _____

NOUN _____

NOUN _____

PLURAL NOUN _____

PART OF THE BODY (PLURAL) _____

NOUN _____

ADVERB _____

Adult
MAD LIBS®

The world's greatest _pride_ game

BACK TO THE WOMYN'S MUSIC FESTIVAL

Hanging with a crowd of womyn born _____ at your local
PLURAL NOUN

_____ music festival is the best way to cap off a summer of
ADJECTIVE

fabulously _____ festivities. Here's how to survive a day at the
ADJECTIVE

_____ Festival:
NOUN

• Stock your cooler with enough _____ to share with your
TYPE OF LIQUID

new _____ .
PLURAL NOUN

• Bring extra cash for T-shirts, handmade _____ , hemp
PLURAL NOUN

bracelets, and local D.I.-_____ . crafts.
LETTER OF THE ALPHABET

• Wear a bra under your _____ . When your
ARTICLE OF CLOTHING

favorite band, _____ and the _____ ,
CELEBRITY (FEMALE) PLURAL NOUN

takes the stage, you'll want to take off your _____ and
NOUN

sing along. Or don't wear a/an _____ at all, you
NOUN

attention-_____ !
NOUN

• On the way home, roll down the _____ and blast your new
PLURAL NOUN

favorite song from the speakers. Hold _____
PART OF THE BODY (PLURAL)

with your girlfriend in the passenger _____ , and vow
NOUN

that you _____ have to come again next year!
ADVERB

Join the millions of Mad Libs fans creating wacky and wonderful stories on our apps!

Download Mad Libs today!